HELPING HUMANITY

Compiled by Vijay from the writings of
Sri Aurobindo and the Mother

SRI AUROBINDO SOCIETY
Pondicherry

Yoga in Everyday Life – Booklet Series

ISBN 81-7060-114-2

First Centenary Edition: 1972
Fourth Revised Edition: 1996

Published by Sri Aurobindo Society, Pondicherry
Printed in India at Sri Aurobindo Ashram Press, Pondicherry

This is one in a series of thirty booklets published by the Sri Aurobindo Society under the title "Yoga in Everyday Life." Our effort is to bring together, from Sri Aurobindo and the Mother, simple passages with a practical orientation on specific subjects, so that everyone may feel free to choose a book according to his inner need. The topics cover the whole field of human activity, because true spirituality is not the rejection of life but the art of perfecting life.

While the passages from Sri Aurobindo are in the original English, most of the passages from the Mother (selections from her talks and writings) are translations from the original French. We must also bear in mind that the excerpts have been taken out of their original context and that a compilation, in its very nature, is likely to have a personal and subjective approach. A sincere attempt, however, has been made to be faithful to the vision of Sri Aurobindo and the Mother.

We hope these booklets will inspire the readers to go to the complete works and will help them to mould their lives and their enviornments towards an ever greater perfection. The quotations from Sri Aurobindo are prefaced by his symbol and those from the Mother by her symbol.

The Mother's

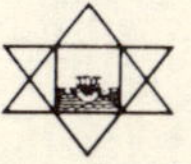

Sri Aurobindo's

"O TRUTH, COME, MANIFEST."

"आयाहि सत्य आविर्भव"

CONTENTS

SERVING HUMANITY

 This is a miracle that men can love God, yet fail to love humanity. With whom are they in love then?

*

 If thou canst not love the vilest worm and the foulest of criminals, how canst thou believe that thou hast accepted God in thy spirit?

To love God, excluding the world, is to give Him an intense but imperfect adoration.

*

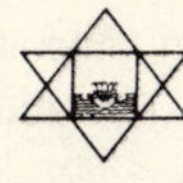 He who has done even a little good to human beings, though he be the worst of sinners, is accepted by God in the ranks of His lovers and servants. He shall look upon the face of the Eternal.

*

(Based on a talk by the Mother)

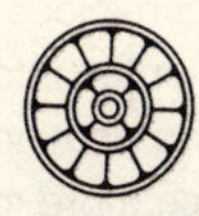 It is easy and comfortable to go within and in an inner consciousness find and maintain a union, even a close union, with the Divine. It is because of such a state of peace and bliss that many, nay, most who go there do not want to come back to normal life upon this earth. And teachers, great or small, almost invariably, have taught that in the end it is best like that, and perhaps the only thing to do under the circumstances. For this life and this earth mean the very opposite of that inner heaven and that highest

good. But some are not given this comfortable solution of the difficulty. They are asked to turn back and live the life of the earth. They are not allowed to remain cosy in a narrow room and be busy always with themselves alone. Indeed, is it not narrow egoism to seek only one's own salvation? When one has saved himself, is it not his duty – the logical outcome and implication of his personal freedom – that he should seek to help others in their salvation? Such was in fact the attitude of the Amitabha Buddha.

A house is on fire. It has a tarred roof. One can easily understand the fury of the fire. Some inmates who were trapped have managed to come out in time, although somewhat bruised and scalded. But there were others, some children, left inside. One of those who came out rushes back again through the flames and comes and goes till all are saved. He is badly burnt, he has risked his life: he did not mind and could not remain at a safe distance. He could not be contented with saving himself, which was to be sure a sufficient gain in one respect. This soul had a consciousness of his wider self.

In the same way, there are souls that have emerged out of the fire of earthly life and are enjoying the safety and security of the heavens; but they have been called to come back into the world, add to the experience of the tranquil above the experience of the trouble below. Surely it increases the scope of their conscious-ness. But to turn upon the world means also to re-enter into ignorance, for this world means ignorance; as it is, it is nothing but ignorance. The role then of one who returns is once more to embrace ignorance, but with a view to bringing into it the light and bliss that he gained from above, permeating the stuff of the present world with the substance of the higher consciousness. It is a sacrifice demanded of him, thus to abandon the eternal felicity of the high heavens – the unbroken union with the Divine above – and to enter into the depths of "this great perilous world": but this is a privilege too, to bring solace to the afflicted, the transforming light to obscure souls, the radiant energy to inert earth. It is a high privilege for which the luminous soul is thankful: he modestly accepts a gift of grace from the Supreme. He accepts the Ignorance and offers it: he lays it at the feet of the Supreme so that it may be transmuted into light – light here below. His own role is that of a modest intermediary.

TWO APOSTLES OF PHILANTHROPY

...I want to tell you about two striking examples chosen from among the adepts of true philanthropy.

Two outstanding beings at the two extremes of thought and action, two of the finest human souls expressing themselves in sensitive and compassionate hearts, received the same psychic shock when they came into contact with the misery of men. Both devoted their whole lives to finding the remedy for the suffering of their fellow-men, and both believed they had found it. But because their solutions, which may be described as contraries, were each in its own domain incomplete and partial, both of them failed to relieve the suffering of humanity.

One in the East, Prince Siddhartha, later known as the Buddha, and the other in the West, Monsieur Vincent, who came to be called Saint Vincent de Paul after his death, stood, so to say, at the two poles of human consciousness, and their methods of assistance were diametrically opposite. Yet both believed in salvation through the spirit, through the Absolute, unknowable to thought, which one called God and the other Nirvana.

Vincent de Paul had an ardent faith and preached to his flock that one must save one's soul. But on coming into contact with human misery, he soon discovered that in order to find one's soul one must have time to look for it. And when do those who labour from morning till night and often from night till morning to eke out a living really have time to think of their souls? So in the simplicity of his charitable heart he concluded that if the poor were at least assured of the barest necessities by those who possess more than they need, these unfortunate people would have enough leisure to lead a better life. He believed in the virtue and efficacy of social work, of active and material charity. He believed that misery could be cured by the multiplication of individual cures, by bringing relief to a greater number, to a very large number of individuals. But this is only a palliative, not a cure. The fullness of consecration, self-abnegation and courage with which he carried on his work has made of him one of the most beautiful and touching figures in human history. And yet his endeavour seems to have rather multiplied than diminished the number of the destitute and the helpless. Certainly the most positive result of his apostleship was to create an appreciable sense of charity in the mentality of a certain section of the well-to-do. And because of this, the work was truly more useful to those who were giving charity than to those who were the object of this charity.

At the other extreme of consciousness stands the Buddha with his pure and sublime compassion. For him the suffering arising out of life could only be abolished by the abolition of life; for life and the world are the outcome of the desire to be, the fruit of ignorance. Abolish desire, eliminate ignorance, and the world will disappear and with it all suffering and misery. In a great effort of spiritual aspiration and silent concentration he elaborated his discipline, one of the most uplifting and the most effective disciplines ever given to those who are eager for liberation.

Millions have believed in his doctrine, although the number of individuals capable of putting it into practice has been very small. But the condition of the earth has remained practically the same and there has been no appreciable diminution in the mass of human suffering.

However, men have canonised the first and deified the second in their attempt to express their gratitude and admiration. But very few have sincerely tried to put into practice the lesson and example that were given to them, although that is truly the only effective way of showing one's gratitude. And yet, even if that had been done, the conditions of human life would not have been perceptibly improved. For to help is not the same as to cure, nor is escaping the same as conquering. Indeed, to alleviate physical hardships, the solution proposed by Vincent de Paul can in no way be enough to cure humanity of its misery and suffering, for not all human sufferings come from physical destitution and can be cured by material means – far from it. Bodily well-being does not inevitably bring peace and joy; and poverty is not necessarily a cause of misery, as is shown by the voluntary poverty of the ascetics of all countries and all ages, who found in their destitution the source and condition of a perfect peace and happiness. Whereas on the contrary, the enjoyment of worldly possessions, of all that material wealth can provide in the way of comfort and pleasure and external satisfaction is powerless to prevent one who possesses these things from suffering pain and sorrow.

Neither can the other solution, escape, the solution of the Buddha, present a practical remedy to the problem. For even if we suppose that a very large number of individuals are capable of practising the discipline and achieving the final liberation, this can in no way abolish suffering from earth and cure others of it, all the others who are still incapable of following the path that leads to Nirvana.

THE MEANING OF CHARITY

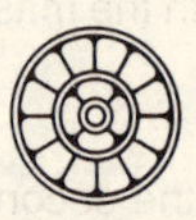...charity, like all other human activities, is exercised according to four different modes which must be simultaneous if its action is to be integral and truly effective. I mean that no charity is complete if it is not at the same time material, intellectual, spiritual or moral and, above all, loving, for the very essence of charity is love.

At present charity is considered almost exclusively from the external standpoint and the word is synonymous with the sharing of part of one's possessions with life's rejects. We shall see in a moment how mean this conception is even when confined to the purely material field.

The three other modes of action of charity are admirably summed up in this counsel given by the Buddha to his disciples: "With your hearts overflowing with compassion, go forth into this world torn by pain, be instructors, and wherever the darkness of ignorance rules, there light a torch." To instruct those who know less, to give to those who do evil the strength to come out of their error, to console those who suffer, these are all occupations of charity, rightly understood. Thus charity, regarded from the individual point of view, consists, for each one, of giving to others all they need, in proportion to one's means.

This brings us to two observations. The first is that one cannot give what one does not have at one's command. Materially this is so evident that it is unnecessary to insist upon it. But intellectually, spiritually, the same rule holds true. Indeed, how can one teach others what one does not know? How can one guide the weak on the path of wisdom if one does not tread the path oneself? How can one radiate love if one does not possess it within oneself?

And the supreme charity, which is integral self-giving to the great work of terrestrial regeneration, implies first of all that one can command what one wants to offer, that is to say, that one is master of oneself. Only he who has perfect self-control can consecrate himself in all sincerity to the great work. For he alone knows that no contrary will, no unexpected impulse can ever again come to impede his action, to check his effort by setting him at variance with himself.

In this fact we find the justification of the old proverb which says: "Charity begins at home." This maxim seems to encourage every kind of egoism, and yet it is the expression of a great wisdom for one who understands it rightly. It is because charitable people fail to conform to this principle that their efforts so often remain unfruitful, that their good-will is so often warped in its results, and that, in the end, they are forced to renounce a charity which, because it has not been rightly exercised, is the cause of nothing but confusion, suffering and disillusionment.

There is evidently a wrong way of interpreting this maxim, which says, "First let us accumulate fortune, intelligence, health, love, energies of all kinds, then we shall distribute them." For, from the material standpoint, when will the accumulation stop? One who acquires the habit of piling up never finds his pile big enough. I have even been led to make an observation about this: that in most men generosity seems to exist in inverse proportion to their pecuniary resources.

From observing the way in which workmen, the needy and all the unfortunate act among themselves, I was forced to conclude that the poor are far more charitable, far more prepared to succour their fellow-sufferers than are those more favoured by fortune. There is not enough time to go into the details of all that I have seen, but I assure you that it is instructive. I can, in any case, assure you that if the rich, in proportion to what they have, gave as much as the poor, soon there would no longer be a single starving person in the world.

Thus gold seems to attract gold, and nothing would be more fatal than wanting to accumulate riches before distributing them. But also, nothing would be more fatal than a rash prodigality which, from lack of discernment, would squander a fortune without benefiting anyone.

Let us never confuse disinterestedness, which is one of the conditions of true charity, with a lack of concern that springs from idle thoughtlessness. Let us learn therefore to make judicious use of what we may have or earn while giving the least possible play to our personality and, above all, let us not forget that charity should not be confined to material aid.

Nor in the field of forces is it possible to accumulate, for receptivity occurs in proportion to expenditure: the more one expends usefully, the more one makes oneself capable of receiving. Thus the intelligence one can acquire is proportionate to the intelligence one uses. We are formed to manifest a certain quantity of intellectual forces, but if we develop ourselves mentally, if we put our brains to work, if we meditate regularly and above all if we make others benefit by the fruit, however modest, of our efforts, we make ourselves capable of receiving a greater quantity of ever deeper and purer intellectual forces. And the same holds true for love and spirituality.

We are like channels: if we do not allow what they have received to pour out freely, not only do they become blocked and no longer receive anything, but what they contain will spoil. If, on the contrary, we allow all this flood of vital, intellectual and spiritual forces to flow abundantly, if by impersonalising ourselves we know how to connect our little individuality to the great universal current, what we give will be returned to us a hundred-fold. To know how not to cut ourselves off from the great universal current, to be a link in the chain which must not be broken, this is the true science, the very key of charity.

Unfortunately there exists a very widespread error which is a serious obstacle to the practical application of this knowledge. This error lies in the belief that a thing in the universe may be our own possession. Everything belongs to all, and to say or think, "This is mine", is to create a separation, a division which does not exist in reality. Everything belongs to all, even the substance of which we are made, a whirl of atoms in perpetual movement which momentarily constitutes our organism without abiding in it and which, tomorrow, will form another.

It is true that some people command great material possessions. But in order to be in accord with the universal law, they should consider themselves as trustees, stewards of these possessions. They ought to know that these riches are entrusted to them so that they may administer them for the best interests of all.

We have come a long way from the narrow conception of charity restricted to the giving of a little of what we have in excess to the unfortunate ones that life brings in our way! And what we say of material riches must be said of spiritual wealth also. Those who say, "This idea is mine", and who think they are very charitable in allowing others to profit from it, are senseless. The world of ideas belongs to all; intellectual force is a universal force.

It is true that some people are more capable than others of entering into relation with this field of ideas and manifesting it through their conscious cerebrality. But this is nothing other than an additional responsibility for them: since they are in possession of this wealth, they are its stewards and must see that it is used for the good of the greatest number. The same holds true for all the other universal forces. Only the concept of union, of the perfect identity of everything and everyone, can lead to true charity.

But to come back to practice, there is one more serious pitfall in the way of its complete and fruitful manifestation. For most people, charity consists of giving anything to anyone without even knowing whether this gift corresponds to a need. Thus charity is made synonymous with sentimental weakness and irrational squandering.

Nothing is more contrary to the very essence of this virtue. Indeed, to give someone a thing he has no need of is as great a lack of charity as to deny him what he needs. And this applies to the things of the spirit as well as to those of the body.

By a faulty distribution of material possessions one can hasten the downfall of certain individuals by encouraging them to be lazy, instead of favouring their progress by inciting them to effort. The same holds true for intelligence and love. To give someone a knowledge which is too strong for him, thoughts which he cannot assimilate, is to deprive him for long, if not for ever, of the possibility of thinking for himself. In the same way, to impose on some people an affection, a love for which they feel no need, is to make them carry a burden which is often too heavy for their shoulders.

This error has two main causes to which all the others can be linked: ignorance and egoism. In order to be sure that an act is beneficial one must know its immediate or distant consequences, and an act of charity is no exception to this law. To want to do well is not enough, one must also know. How much evil has been done in the world in the name of charity diverted from its true sense and completely warped in its results! I could give you many examples of acts of charity which have led to the most disastrous results because they were performed without reflection, without dicernment, without understanding, without insight.

Charity, like all things, must be the result in us of a conscious and reasoned will, for impulse is synonymous with error and above all with egoism.

Unfortunately it must be acknowledged that charity is very seldom completely disinterested. I do not mean charity which is performed for the purpose of acquiring merit in the eyes of a personal God or to win eternal bliss. This utterly base form is the worst of all bargainings and to call it charity would be to tarnish this name. But I mean charity which is performed because one finds pleasure in it and which is still subject to all kidns of likes or dislikes, attractions or repulsions. That kind of charity is very rarely completely free from the desire to meet with gratitude, and such a desire always atrophies the impartial clear-sighted-ness which is necessary to any action if it is to have its full value.

There is a wisdom in charity as everywhere, and it is to reduce waste to the minimum. Thus to be truly charitable one must be impersonal. And once more we see that all the lines of human progress converge on the same necessity: self-mastery, dying to oneself in order to be born into the new and true life. To the extent that we outgrow the habit of referring everything to ourselves, we can exercise a truly effective charity, a charity one with love.

Besides, there is a height where all virtues meet in communion:

love, goodness, compassion, forbearance, charity are all one and the same in their essence. From this point of view, charity could be considered as the tangible and practical outer action determined by the application of the virtues of love. For there is a force which can be distributed to all, always, provided that it is given in its most impersonal form: this is love, love which contains within itself light and life, that is, all the possibilities of intelligence, health, blossoming.

Yes, there is a sublime charity, one which rises from a happy heart, from a serene soul. One who has won inner peace is a herald of deliverance wherever he goes, a bearer of hope and joy. Is not this what poor and suffering humanity needs above all things?

Yes, there are certain men whose thoughts are all love, who radiate love, and the mere presence of these individuals is a charity more active, more real than any other. Though they utter no word and make no gesture, yet the sick are relieved, the tormented are soothed, the ignorant are enlightened, the wicked are appeased, those who suffer are consoled and all undergo this deep transformation which will open new horizons to them, enable them to take a step forward which no doubt will be decisive, on the infinite path of progress. These individuals who, out of love, give themselves to all, who become the servants of all, are the living symbols of the supreme Charity.

ALTRUISM AS A FORM OF THE EGO

When I see others suffer, I feel that I am unfortunate, but the wisdom that is not mine, sees the good that is coming and approves.

Selfishness kills the soul; destroy it. But take care that your altruism does not kill the souls of others.

Very usually, altruism is only the sublimest form of selfishness.

Altruism is good for man, but less good when it is a form of supreme self-indulgence and lives by pampering the selfishness of others.

By altruism thou canst save thy soul, but see that thou save it not by indulging in the perdition of thy brother.

Pity may be reserved, so long as thy soul makes distinctions, for the suffering animals; but humanity deserves from thee something nobler, it asks for love, for understanding, for comradeship, for the help of the equal and brother.

That thou shouldst have pity on creatures is well, but not well, if thou art a slave to thy pity. Be a slave to nothing except to God, not even to His most luminous angels.

To find that saving a man's body or mind from suffering is not always for the good of either soul, mind or body is one of the bitterest of experiences for the humanly compassionate.

Human pity is born of ignorance and weakness; it is the slave of emotional impressions. Divine compassion understands, discerns and saves.

Pity is sometimes a good substitute for love; but it is always no more than a substitute.

Self-pity is always born of self-love; but pity for others is not always born of love for its object. It is sometimes a self-regarding shrinking from the sight of pain; sometimes the rich man's contemptuous dole to the pauper. Develop rather God's divine compassion than human pity.

Not pity that bites the heart and weakens the inner members, but a divine masterful and untroubled compassion and help-fulness is the virtue that we should encourage.

Love and serve men, but beware lest thou desire their appro-bation. Obey rather God within thee.

*

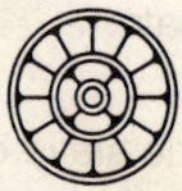 *How can "altruism, duty, family, country, humanity" become true instruments of the soul?*

The soul belongs to the Divine, and owes obe-dience and service to the Divine alone. If the Divine commands it to work for family, country or humanity, then it is all right and it can do so without being imprisoned.

If the command does not come from the Divine, to serve these things is only to obey social and moral conventions.

*

"One of the commonest forms of ambition is the idea of service to humanity. All attachment to such service or work is a sign of personal ambition."

Why do you say that this is ambition?

Why do you want to serve humanity, what is your idea? It is ambition, it is in order to become a great man among men. It is difficult to understand?...

The Divine is everywhere. So if one serves humanity, one serves the Divine, isn't that so?

That's marvellous! The clearest thing in this business is to say:

"The Divine is in me. If I serve myself, I am also serving the Divine!" In fact, the Divine is everywhere. The Divine will do His own work very well without you.

I see quite well that you do not understand. But truly, if you do understand that the Divine is there, in all things, with what are you meddling in serving humanity? To serve humanity you must know better than the Divine what must be done for it. Do you know better than the Divine how to serve it?

The Divine is everywhere. Yes. Things don't seem to be divine.... As for me, I see only one solution: if you want to help humanity, there is only one thing to do, it is to take yourself as completely as possible and offer yourself to the Divine. That is the solution. Because in this way, at least the material reality which you represent will be able to grow a little more like the Divine.

We are told that the Divine is in all things. Why don't things change? Because the Divine does not get a response, everything does not respond to the Divine. One must search the depths of the consciousness to see this. What do you want to do to serve humanity? Give food to the poor? – You can feed millions of them. That will not be a solution, this problem will remain the same. Give new and better living conditions to men? – The Divine is in them, how is it that things don't change? The Divine must know better than you the condition of humanity. What are you? You represent only a little bit of consciousness and a little bit of matter, it is that you call "myself". If you want to help humanity, the world or the universe, the only thing to do is to give that little bit entirely to the Divine. Why is the world not divine?... It is evident that the world is not in order. So the only solution to the problem is to give what belongs to you. Give it totally, entirely to the Divine; not only for yourself but for humanity, for the universe. There is no better solution. How do you want to help humanity? You don't even know what it needs. Perhaps you know still less what power you are serving. How can you change anything without indeed having changed yourself?

In any case, you are not powerful enough to do it. How do you expect to help another if you do not have a higher consciousness than he? It is such a childish idea! It is children who say: "I am opening a boarding-house, I am going to build a crèche, give soup to the poor, preach this knowledge, spread this religion...." It is only because you consider yourself better than others, think you know better than they what they should be or do. That's what it is, serving humanity. You want to continue all that? It has not changed things much. It is not to help humanity that one opens a hospital or a school.

All the same it has helped, hasn't it? If all the schools were abolished...

I don't think that humanity is happier than it was before nor that there has been a great improvement. All this mostly gives you the feeling "I am something." That's what I call ambition.

If these very people who are ready to give money for schools were told that there was a divine Work to be done, that the Divine has decided to do it in this particular way, even if they are convinced that it is indeed the Divine's Work, they refuse to give anything, for this is not a recognised form of beneficence – one doesn't have the satisfaction of having done something good! This is what I call ambition. I had instances of people who could give lakhs of rupees to open a hospital, for that gives them the satisfaction of doing something great, noble, generous. They glorify themselves, that's what I call ambition.

16

I knew a humorist who used to say: "It won't be so soon that the kingdom of God will come, for those poor philanthropists – what would remain for them? If humanity suffered no longer, the philanthropists would be without work." It is difficult to come out of that. However, it is a fact that never will the world come out of the state in which it is unless it gives itself up to the Divine. All the virtues – you may glorify them – increase your self-satisfaction, that is, your ego; they do not help you truly to become aware of the Divine. It is the generous and wise people of this world who are the most difficult to convert. They are very satisfied with their life. A poor fellow who has done all sorts of stupid things all his life feels immediately sorry and says: "I am nothing, can do nothing. Make of me what You want." Such a one is more right and much closer to the Divine than one who is wise and full of his wisdom and vanity. He sees himself as he is.

The generous and wise man who has done much for humanity is too self-satisfied to have the least idea of changing. It is usually these people who say: "If indeed I had created the world, I wouldn't have made it like this, I would have created it much better than that", and they try to set right what the Divine has done badly! According to their picture, all this is stupid and useless.... It is not with that attitude that you can belong to the Divine. There will always be between you and Him the conscious ego of one's own intellectual superiority which judges the Divine and is sure of never being mistaken. For they are convinced that if they had made the world, they would not have committed all the stupidities that God has perpetrated. And all this comes from pride, vanity, self-conceit; and there is exactly the seed of that in people who want to serve humanity.

What are they going to give to humanity? Nothing at all! Even if they gave every drop of their blood, all the ideas in their head, all the money in their pocket, that could not change one individual, who is but a second of time in eternity. They believe they can serve eternity? There are even beings higher than man who have come, have brought the light, given their life, and that has not changed things much. So how can a little man, a microscopic being, truly help? It is pride. The argument given is: "If everyone did his best, all would go well." I don't think so and, even, it is impossible. In a certain way, each thing in the universe does its best. But that best doesn't come to anything at all. Unless everything changes, nothing will change. It is this best that must change. In the place of ignorance must be born knowledge and power and consciousness, otherwise we shall always turn in a circle around the same stupidity.

You may open millions of hospitals, that will not prevent people getting ill. On the contrary, they will have every facility and encouragement to fall ill. We are steeped in ideas of this kind. This puts your conscience at rest: "I have come to the world, I must help others." One tells oneself: "How disinterested I am! I am going to help humanity." All this is nothing but egoism.

In fact, the first human being that concerns you is yourself. You want to diminish suffering, but unless you can change the capacity of suffering into a certitude of being happy, the world will not change. It will always be the same, we turn in a circle – one civilisation follows another, one catastrophe another; but the thing does not change, for there is something missing, something not there, that is the consciousness. That's all.

At least, that's my opinion. I am giving it to you for what it is worth. If you want to build hospitals, schools, you may do so; if that makes you happy, so much the better for you. It has not much importance. When I saw the film *Monsieur Vincent*, I was very interested. He found out that when he fed ten poor men, a thousand came along. That was what Colbert told him: "It seems you create them, your poor ones, by feeding them!'' And it is not altogether false. However! If it is your destiny to found schools and give instruction, to care for the sick, to open hospitals, it is good, do it. But you must not take that very seriously. It is something grandiose you are doing for your own pleasure. Say: ''I am doing it because it gives me pleasure.'' But do not speak of yoga. It is not yoga you are doing. You believe you are doing something great, that's all, and it is for your personal satisfaction.

*

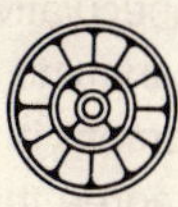

Should one give money to beggars or not?

In a well-organised society, there should not be any beggars.

But as long as there are, do as you feel.

There are good reasons both for doing it and for not doing it.

THE BEST WAY — TO CHANGE ONESELF

To concentrate most on one's own spiritual growth and experience is the first necessity of the sadhak — to be eager to help others draws away from the inner work. To grow in the spirit is the greatest help one can give to others, for then something flows out naturally to those around that helps them.

*

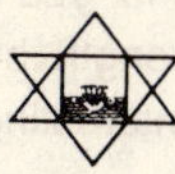

...after all, the best way to make Humanity progress is to move on oneself, – that may sound either individualistic or egoistic, but it isn't: it is only common sense. As the Gita says:

"Whatever the best do is taken as the model by the rest."

There are always unregenerate parts tugging people backwards and who is not divided? But it is best to put one's trust in the soul, the spark of the Divine within, and foster that till it rises into a sufficient flame.

*

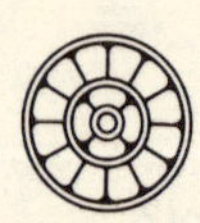 It is like those people in despair who tell you, "Why is the world so frightful?" What is the use of lamenting, since it is like that? The only thing you can do is to work to change it. Naturally, from a speculative point of view one may try to understand, but the human mind is incapable of understanding such things. For the moment it is quite useless. What is useful is to change it. We all agree that the world is detestable, that it is not what it ought to be, and the only thing we have to do is to work to make it otherwise. Consequently, our whole preoccupation should be to find the best means of making it different; and we can understand one thing, it is that the best means (though we do not know it quite well yet), is we ourselves, isn't it? And surely you know yourself better than you know your neighbour – you understand better the consciousness manifested in a human being than that manifested in the stars, for instance. So, after a little hesitation you could say, "After all, the best means is what I am. I don't know very well what I am, but this kind of collection of things that I am, this perhaps is my work, this is perhaps my part of the work, and if I do it as well as I can, perhaps I shall be doing the best I can do." This is a very big beginning, very big. It is not overwhelming, not beyond the limits of your possibilities. You have your work at hand, it is always within your reach, so to say, it is always there for you to attend to it – a field of action proportionate to your strength, but varied enough, complex, vast, deep enough to be interesting. And you explore this unknown world.

Many people tell you, "But then this is egoism!" – it is egoism if you do it in an egoistic way, for your personal profit, if you try to acquire powers, to become powerful enough to influence others, or if you seek means to make a comfortable life for yourself. Naturally, if you do it in this spirit, it will be egoistic. But the beauty of it is that you will not get anywhere! You will begin by deceiving yourself, you will live in increasing illusions and you will fall back into a greater and greater obscurity. Consequently, things are organised much better than one thinks; if you do your work egoistically (we have said that our field of work is always within our reach) it will come to nothing. And hence the required condition is to do it with an absolute sincerity in your aspiration for the realisation of the divine work. So if you start like that I can assure you that you will have such an interesting journey that even if it takes very long, you will never get tired. But you must do it like that with an intensity of will, with perseverance and that indispensable good humour which smiles at difficulties and laughs at mistakes. Then everything will go well.

*

Can one help the world with a vibration of goodwill?

With good wishes one can change many things, only it must be an extremely pure and unmixed goodwill. It is quite obvious that a thought, a perfectly pure and true prayer, if it is sent forth into the world, does its work. But where is this perfectly pure and true thought when it passes into the human brain? There are degradations. If through an effort of inner consciousness and knowledge, you can truly overcome in yourself a desire, that is to say, dissolve and abolish it, and if through inner goodwill, through consciousness, light, knowledge, you are able to dissolve the desire, you will be, first of all in yourself personally, a hundred times happier than if you had satisfied this desire, and then it will have a marvellous effect. It

21

will have a repercussion in the world of which you have no idea. It will spread forth. For the vibrations you have created will continue to spread. These things grow larger like the snowball. The victory you win in your character, however small it be, is one which can be gained in the whole world. And it is this I meant just now: all things which are done outwardly without changing the inner nature – hospitals, schools, etc. – are done through vanity, for the feeling of being great, whilst these small un-noticed things overcome in oneself gain an infinitely greater victory, though the effects are hidden. Every movement in you which is false and opposed to the truth is a negation of the divine life. Your small efforts have considerable results which you don't even have the satisfaction of knowing, but which are true and have precisely an impersonal and general effect.

If you really want to do something good, the best thing you can do is to win your small victories in all sincerity, one after another, and thus you will do for the world the maximum you are able to.

Will our victory act for the whole world?

It will not change the whole world. For your victory is too small for the whole world. Millions of such victories are needed. It is a very small victory if compared with the whole. But it gets mingled with other things.... It could be said that it is like bringing into the world the *capacity* of doing a thing. But for this to act effectively, at times centuries are necessary; it is a question of proportion. You can try it out (and it is much more difficult) even with those around you. You must be absolutely sincere, not do it with the idea of getting a result, but because you want to gain a victory. If you gain it, it will necessarily have an effect on those around you. But if a bargaining element is mixed up in it, if you do this thing because you want to get that other: "I want to overcome my defects, but that person must also overcome his", then that doesn't work. It is a merchant's attitude: "I give this, but I shall take that." That spoils everything. There is neither sincerity nor purity. It is bargaining.

Nothing must be mixed with your sincerity, your aspiration, your motive. You do things for love of the Divine, for truth, for perfection, without any other motive, any other idea. And that brings results.

THE ONLY WAY – A CHANGE OF CONSCIOUSNESS

 Often we see [the] desire of personal salvation overcome by another attraction which also belongs to the higher turn of our nature and which indicates the essential character of the action the liberated soul must pursue. It is that which is implied in the great legend of the Amitabha Buddha who turned away when his spirit was on the threshold of Nirvana and took the vow never to cross it while a single being remained in the sorrow and the Ignorance. It is that which underlies the sublime verse of the Bhagavata Purana, "I desire not the supreme state with all its eight siddhis nor the cessation of rebirth; may I assume the sorrow of all creatures who suffer and enter into them so that they may be made free from grief." It is that which inspires a remarkable passage in a letter of Swami Vivekananda, "I have lost all wish for my salvation," wrote the great Vedantin, "may I be born again and again and suffer thousands of miseries so that I may worship the only God that exists, the only God I believe in, the sum-total of all souls, – and above all, my God the wicked, my God the miserable, my God the poor of all races, of all species is the special object of my worship. He who is the high and low, the saint and the sinner, the god and the worm, Him worship, the visible, the knowable, the real, the omnipresent; break all other idols. In whom there is neither past life nor future birth, nor death nor going nor coming, in whom we always have been and

always will be one, Him worship; break all other idols."

The last two sentences contain indeed the whole gist of the matter. The true salvation or the true freedom from the chain of rebirth is not the rejection of terrestrial life or the individual's escape by a spiritual self-annihilation, even as the true renunciation is not the mere physical abandonment of family and society; it is the inner identification with the Divine in whom there is no limitation of past life and future birth but instead the eternal existence of the unborn Soul.

*

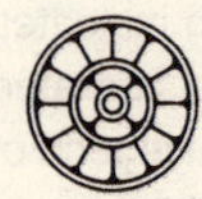 Indeed, true happiness is the happiness one can feel in any circumstances whatsoever, because it comes from regions which cannot be affected by any external circumstances. But this happiness is accessible only to a very few individuals, and most of the human race is still subject to terrestrial conditions. So we can say on one hand that a change in the human consciousness is absolutely indispensable and, on the other, that without an integral transformation of the terrestrial atmosphere, the conditions of human life cannot be effectively changed. In either case, the remedy is the same: a new consciousness must manifest on earth and in man. Only the appearance of a new force and light and power accompanying the descent of the supramental consciousness into this world can raise man out of the anguish and pain and misery in which he is submerged. For only the supramental consciousness bringing down upon earth a higher poise and a purer and truer light can achieve the great miracle of transformation.

Nature is striving towards this new manifestation. But her ways are tortuous and her march is uncertain, full of halts and regressions, so much so that it is difficult to perceive her true plan. However, it is becoming more and more clear that she wants to bring forth a new species out of the human species, a supramental race that will be to man what man is to the animal. But the advent of this transformation, this creation of a new race which Nature would take centuries of groping attempts to bring about, can be effected by the intelligent will of man, not only in a much shorter time but also with much less waste and loss.

Here the integral Yoga has its rightful place and utility. For Yoga is meant to overcome, by the intensity of its concentration and effort, the delay that time imposes on all radical transformation, on all new creation.

The integral Yoga is not an escape from the physical world which leaves it irrevocably to its fate, nor is it an acceptance of material life as it is without any hope of decisive change, or of the world as the final expression of the Divine Will.

The integral Yoga aims at scaling all the degrees of consciousness from the ordinary mental consciousness to a supramental and divine consciousness, and when the ascent is completed, to return to the material world and infuse it with the supramental force and consciousness that have been won, so that this earth may be gradually transformed into a supramental and divine world.

The integral Yoga is especially intended for those who have realised in themselves all that man can realise and yet are not satisfied, for they demand from life what it cannot give. Those who yearn for the unknown and aspire for perfection, who ask themselves agonising questions and have not found any definitive answers to them, they are the ones who are ready for the integral Yoga.

For there is a series of fundamental questions which those who are concerned by the fate of mankind and are not satisfied with current formulas inevitably ask themselves. They can be formulated approximately as follows:

Why is one born if only to die?
Why does one live if only to suffer?
Why does one love if only to be separated?

Why does one think if only to err?
Why does one act if only to make mistakes?

The sole acceptable answer is that things are not what they ought to be and that these contradictions are not only not inevitable but they are rectifiable and will one day disappear. For the world is not irremediably what it is. The earth is in a period of transition that certainly seems long to the brief human consciousness, but which is infinitesimal for the eternal consciousness. And this period will come to an end with the appearance of the supramental consciousness. The contradictions will then be replaced by harmonies and the oppositions by syntheses.

This new creation, the appearance of a superhuman race, has already been the object of much speculation and controversy. It pleases man's imagination to draw more or less flattering portraits of what the superman will be like. But only like can know like, and it is only by becoming conscious of the divine nature in its essence that one will be able to have a conception of what the divine nature will be in the manifestation. Yet those who have realised this consciousness in themselves are usually more anxious to become the superman than to give a description of him.

However, it may be useful to say what the superman will certainly not be, so as to clear away certain misunderstandings. For example, I have read somewhere that the superhuman race would be fundamentally cruel and insensitive; since it is above suffering, it will attach no importance to the suffering of others and will take it as a sign of their imperfection and inferiority. No doubt, those who think in this way are judging the relations between superman and man from the manner in which man behaves towards his lesser brethren, the animals. But such behaviour, far from being a proof of superiority, is a sure sign of unconsciousness and stupidity. This is shown by the fact that as soon as man rises to a little higher level, he begins to feel compassion towards animals and seeks to improve their lot. Yet there is an element of truth in the conception of the unfeeling superman: it is this, that the higher race will not feel the kind of egoistic, weak and sentimental pity which men call charity. This pity, which does more harm than good, will be replaced by a strong and enlightened compassion whose only purpose will be to provide a true remedy to suffering, not to perpetuate it.

On the other hand, this conception describes fairly well what the reign of a race of vital beings upon earth would be like. They are immortal in their nature and much more powerful than man in their capacities, but they are also incurably anti-divine in their will, and their mission in the universe seems to be to delay the divine realisation until the instruments of this realisation, that is to say, men, become pure and strong and perfect enough to overcome all obstacles. It might not perhaps be useless to put the poor afflicted earth on guard against the possibility of such an evil domination.

Until the superman can come in person to show man what his true nature is, it might be wise for every human being of goodwill to become conscious of what he can conceive as the most beautiful, the most noble, the truest and purest, the most luminous and best, and to aspire that this conception may be realised in himself for the greatest good of the world and men.

REFERENCES – HELPING HUMANITY

Booklet
Page

1a	SABCL Vol. 17, p. 84	14b	MCW Vol. 5, pp. 12-16
b	SABCL Vol. 17, p. 133	19a	MCW Vol. 16, p. 407
c	SABCL Vol. 17, p. 143	b	SABCL Vol. 22, p. 151
d	NKGCW Vol. 3, pp. 268-69	c	SABCL Vol. 22, pp. 150-51
3	MCW Vol. 12, pp. 95-97	20	MCW Vol. 4, pp. 253-54
6	MCW Vol. 2, pp. 95-102	21	MCW Vol. 5, pp. 19-21
12	SABCL Vol. 17, pp. 81-145	23	SABCL Vol. 20, pp. 257-58
14a	MCW Vol. 10, p. 285	24	MCW Vol. 12, pp. 97-101

N.B. Abbreviations: SABCL – Sri Aurobindo Birth Centenary Library
MCW – Mother's Collected Works
NKGCW – Nolini Kanta Gupta's Collected Works
The quotation in the last line of the introduction is from 'White Roses'.